Rethink Your New Year Goals

Rethink Your New Year Goals

Alex's 7-Day Challenge to Patience and Perseverance

Liudmila Pirojenko

Table of Contents

Introduction: Why New Year Goals Matter

AS THE CALENDAR flips to a new year, we are given a unique opportunity to reflect, recalibrate, and recommit ourselves to the visions we hold for our lives. New Year's goals serve as guiding stars, illuminating our path and providing focus amidst the chaos of everyday life. They compel us to look inward, confront our aspirations, and embrace the potential for change and growth. However, setting goals extends beyond mere resolutions; it is an essential part of the human experience that shapes our identity, fuels our motivations, and contributes to our overall well-being.

Goals give our lives direction and purpose. Without them, life can feel aimless, like a ship adrift at sea without a destination. Many of us have experienced the ache that accompanies stagnation—moments when the days blend into a monotonous routine, and we drift through life without feeling any sense of achievement or fulfillment. This is more than an emotional state; it can lead to dissatisfaction, frustration, and hopelessness. When we lack objectives to strive for, we often grapple with an unsettling void—a disconnect between our current realities and the life we envisioned for ourselves.

Living without goals can inhibit our growth and development. Humans are innately driven to evolve, both personally and professionally. Setting goals encourages us to challenge our limits, develop new skills, and step outside our comfort zones. When we do not give ourselves something to strive for, we miss opportunities to stretch our capabilities, learn from our experiences, and ultimately cultivate resilience. This absence of ambition can leave us languishing in mediocrity—an exhausting place where dreams simmer quietly while life passes us by.

New Year's goals are particularly significant because they symbolize renewal and hope. As we end one year and welcome another, we are offered a collective moment to shed the burdens of the past and envision a brighter future. This transition acts as a natural checkpoint in our lives, inviting us to assess where we stand and where we wish to go. Whether pursuing a new career, enhancing personal relationships, improving health, or nurturing a long-held passion, the turning of the year presents a fresh slate, a chance to redefine our aspirations.

Setting and working towards goals fosters a sense of accountability. When we commit to a goal, we are not just making a promise to ourselves but laying the groundwork for a brighter future. Sharing our goals with friends, family, or a community creates a layer of commitment, inviting support and encouragement. This social aspect is vital; it reminds us that we are not alone in our journey. Pursuing our goals can inspire others to embark on their journeys, creating a ripple effect of motivation and positivity.

Manifesting our goals cultivates patience and perseverance— key ingredients for success. Too often want instant results but forget that meaningful change takes time. In this age of rapid gratification, we may become disheartened when things don't unfold as quickly as we'd like. However, understanding that challenges and setbacks are part of the journey can empower us to stay the course, develop resilience, and embrace the learning experiences that accompany growth.

"Alex's 7-Day Challenge to Patience and Perseverance" is designed to take you on a transformative expedition as we delve dinto the core of meaningful goal-setting.

This guide will equip you with practical tools and insights to help you cultivate the mindset needed to achieve your New Year goals. Embrace patience and perseverance, and you'll be better prepared to face challenges and learn to appreciate the journey itself. In a world where change is the only constant, committing to your goals can be the anchor that keeps you grounded while navigating the waves of life.

Let's embark on this journey and unlock your potential to create your desired life. The first step begins now, and your future self will thank you.

Day 1: Recognition

Story:

ALEX is a young professional navigating the tumultuous waters of adulthood. Today, he stepped out of his office, his heart heavy with frustration. His boss, visibly stressed and on edge, had taken it out on him, making snide remarks and dismissing his contributions. As Alex walked to his car, he couldn't shake off the feeling of inadequacy from the confrontation. The job he once found fulfilling now felt like a source of constant anxiety.

Later, Alex had planned to meet his girlfriend, Mia, hoping that spending time together would lift his spirits. However, when he arrived, he found her overwhelmed with her problems. Mia was juggling work deadlines, family issues, and her feelings of self-doubt. Instead of the comforting embrace he had anticipated, their conversation quickly spiraled into a quarrel. Frustrated by her inability to see his struggles and feeling unsupported, Alex left the conversation feeling even more isolated.

As he sat alone in his car, the day's weight began to settle in. He felt overwhelmed by his challenges—not just at work but also in his personal life. The stress was palpable, and self-doubt crept in, whispering that he wasn't good enough and was failing in his career and relationship.

At that moment of solitude, Alex realized he needed to step back and recognize the importance of patience and perseverance. Life threw obstacles his way, but he could choose how to respond. He understood that these challenges were not insurmountable but opportunities for growth provided he approached them with the right mindset.

Exercise:

Now it's your turn to reflect on your challenges and how patience and perseverance can help you navigate them. Take a moment to write down three current challenges you are facing. Consider what patience and perseverance might look like for each challenge in that context.

Challenge 1: Job Stress

- Patience. I recognize that not every day will be perfect and that setbacks are okay. I allow myself the time to learn and grow from difficult experiences rather than expecting immediate results.
- Perseverance. I'm committing to improving my skills and seeking solutions to my work issues, whether that means asking for help, pursuing additional training, or finding ways to manage stress effectively.

Challenge 2: Relationship Issues

- Patience. I understand that every relationship goes through rough patches, and it is important for me to listen and communicate openly with my partner. This allows space for both of us to express our feelings without judgment.

- ○ Perseverance. Working through conflicts together, seeking to understand each other's perspectives, and committing to finding solutions rather than giving up when things get tough.

Challenge 3: Self-Doubt

- ○ Patience. I should acknowledge that overcoming self-doubt takes time. I should be kind to myself and accept that sometimes, feeling uncertain is normal.
- ○ Perseverance. I actively challenge negative thoughts by focusing on my strengths and accomplishments. I set small, achievable goals to build my confidence and gradually overcome my insecurities.

Recognize your challenges and identify how patience and perseverance can help you overcome them. You are taking the first step on your journey towards personal growth. Remember, it's not about avoiding difficulties but learning to navigate them with resilience and grace.

Day 2: Setting Intentions

Story:

AS DAWN BROKE, Alex felt a renewed sense of purpose on the second day of his journey. The previous day's frustrations were still fresh in his mind, but instead of allowing them to overwhelm him, he decided it was time to take ownership of his situation. He realized that while he couldn't control everything around him, he could control his responses and the mindset he adopted moving forward.

Sitting at his kitchen table with a cup of coffee, Alex took a moment to breathe deeply. The morning's tranquility starkly contrasted with the chaos of the past few days. He grabbed his journal, a companion he had neglected for far too long, and began to write.

After some reflection, Alex composed his intention for the week: "I will embrace challenges and develop resilience." This simple yet powerful statement was a guiding light, reminding him of his commitment to cultivating patience and perseverance in every aspect of his life.

Alex couldn't help but think about previous experiences where these qualities had made a significant difference. He remembered a time during college when he struggled with a particularly tough exam. Faced with anxiety and self-doubt, he focused on staying patient, studying diligently, and believing in his ability to succeed. He passed the exam and learned valuable lessons about hard work and perseverance that have carried over into other areas of his life.

With this memory as his motivation, Alex felt a surge of determination. He recognized that setting intentions would keep him accountable and empower him to face the week ahead positively. He took a deep breath and began to list specific goals to work on this week, each rooted in his challenges and his newfound intention.

Exercise
Create an Intention Statement and Goals
Intention Statement
"I will embrace challenges and develop resilience."

Goals for the Week

Goal 1: Improve Job Performance
- Action Step: I will dedicate at least 30 minutes daily to professional development through online courses or reading articles related to my field.
- Patience Focus: Understanding that improvement takes time and it's okay to make mistakes along the way.

Goal 2: Foster Better Communication with My Girlfriend
- Action Step: Schedule a "check-in" conversation with Mia this week to discuss our feelings and challenges without distractions.
- Perseverance Focus: Committing to approaching difficult conversations with empathy and a willingness to listen, even when it feels uncomfortable.

Goal 3: Overcome Self-Doubt
- Action Step: Write down three accomplishments daily to
- remind myself of my abilities and strengths, and reflect on them with gratitude.

Patience Focus: Allowing myself to recognize that building confidence is gradual and embracing each small success.

Goal 4: Manage Stress Effectively
- Action Step: Practice daily mindfulness, such as meditation or deep breathing exercises, for at least ten minutes.
- Perseverance Focus: Consistently integrating mindfulness into my routine, even on stressful days, to build my resilience over time.
-

Goal 5: Cultivate a Positive Mindset
- Action Step: Start a gratitude journal and write down three things I am grateful for daily.
- Patience Focus: Understanding that developing a positive mindset may take time and being kind to myself when it's harder to see the good.

Setting these intentions and goals helped Alex pave the way for a more intentional and resilient approach to life's challenges. Each step he took brought him closer to facing his difficulties and thriving despite them. With his intention statement as a cornerstone, he was ready to embrace whatever the week had in store, equipped with patience and perseverance.

An intentional and resilient approach to life's challenges is about actively choosing how to respond to adversity rather than reacting at the moment out of habit or emotional impulse. This mindset allows individuals to navigate difficulties with clarity, purpose, and strength. Here's a deeper look at what it means to adopt such an approach, particularly in the context of Alex's journey.

Intentionality in Life's Challenges

Setting Clear Intentions

Intentionality starts with establishing clear intentions. Alex's intention to embrace challenges and develop resilience became a guiding principle. This clarity helps him focus on what truly matters, allowing him to filter out distractions and emotional responses that do not serve his goals. Setting intentions provides a powerful anchor during turbulent times, reminding him of his purpose and values.

Mindful Decision-Making

An intentional approach encourages mindfulness in decision-making. Instead of reacting impulsively to challenges, Alex learned to pause and reflect on how he wanted to respond. This reflection process enables him to gather his thoughts, consider potential outcomes, and choose actions that align with his goals and values. Whether it's navigating a difficult conversation with Mia or managing stress at work, mindful decision-making empowers him to respond thoughtfully.

Prioritizing Growth Over Comfort

Adopting an intentional mindset often means prioritizing growth over comfort. Challenges are inherently uncomfortable, but Alex recognizes that stepping out of his comfort zone is essential for personal development. By intentionally facing difficulties at work or in his relationships, he embraces the opportunity to learn and grow, transforming discomfort into a catalyst for resilience.

Resilience in the Face of Challenges

Embracing Change

Resilience involves accepting that change is an inevitable part of life. Through his experiences, Alex learned that both anticipated and unforeseen changes can disrupt stability. Instead of resisting change or becoming overwhelmed, he embraced it, recognizing that it often leads to new opportunities and perspectives. This flexibility enhances his ability to adapt and thrive when faced with unexpected situations.

Fostering a Positive Mindset

Resilience is closely tied to maintaining a positive outlook, even during trying times. Alex's commitment to gratitude and self-reflection nurtures a mindset that focuses on possibilities rather than limitations. By looking for lessons in each challenge, he cultivates an optimistic view, empowering him to see setbacks as temporary and surmountable.

Building a Supportive Network

Resilience is not just an individual endeavor; it thrives in a supportive environment. Alex recognized the importance of surrounding himself with encouraging friends and family throughout his journey. By communicating openly about his challenges and seeking support when needed, he fostered connections that bolstered his resilience. This support system provides encouragement and perspective when he faces difficulties, reminding him that he is not alone.

Developing Coping Strategies

A resilient approach includes developing a toolbox of coping strategies to navigate stress and challenges. For Alex, this involved integrating mindfulness practices, like meditation and deep breathing, into his daily routine. These techniques help him manage anxiety and remain centered, enabling him to approach challenges with a calm and clear mindset.

Practicing Self-Compassion

Resilience flourishes with self-compassion. Alex learned to treat himself kindly in the face of setbacks and self-doubt. Instead of criticizing himself for perceived failures, he recognized that everyone encounters difficulties and that growth often stems from these moments. Practicing self-compassion allows him to bounce back faster from disappointments and maintain a motivation to keep moving forward.

The Synergy of Intention and Resilience

Intentionality and resilience create a powerful framework for navigating life's challenges. An intentional mindset fuels resilience by providing purpose and direction. When faced with obstacles, Alex can draw on his intentions to remain steadfast and committed to his personal growth. Conversely, resilience enhances his capacity to live intentionally, empowering him to endure setbacks with strength and determination.

A Continuous Path

An intentional and resilient approach to life is not a destination but a continuous journey. Each challenge Alex faces allows him to practice intention and resilience, reinforcing his skills and character.

As he becomes more adept at handling adversity, he cultivates a deeper understanding of himself and the world around him. This journey transforms challenges into vital learning experiences, equipping him with the tools to face future obstacles with greater confidence and grace.

With this approach, Alex navigates his challenges more effectively and helps inspire those around him, contributing to a shared sense of strength and purpose in their collective experiences.

Day 3: Daily Mindfulness

Story:

AS DAY 3 of his journey unfolded, Alex felt a sense of anticipation. He had committed to integrating mindfulness into his daily routine, believing that increased self-awareness would pave the way for greater patience and resilience. He set the intention to start each day with a short mindfulness practice, understanding that even a few minutes could help ground him amidst life's challenges.

After a fulfilling breakfast, Alex visited his local coffee shop before heading to work. He looked forward to enjoying his favorite brew and taking a moment to appreciate the little things. However, as he entered the café, a long line greeted him, stretching far beyond what he had anticipated. His initial excitement waned, and impatience threatened to seep in.

As he waited, he caught sight of his watch, feeling the pressure of time ticking away. He could feel frustration bubbling beneath the surface, especially as he noticed the barista moving slower than usual. Thoughts raced through his mind: "Why don't they speed things up? I'll be late for work!"

At that moment of agitation, he remembered his intention to cultivate mindfulness. Instead of letting frustration take over, Alex paused. He recalled the breathing techniques he had read about the previous day and decided to put them into practice. He found a quiet corner of the café and closed his eyes momentarily. With each breath, he focused on the present, letting go of the impatience that threatened to consume him.

Exercise: Practice a 5-Minute Mindfulness Meditation

To help you cultivate this practice, take a moment to engage in a brief mindfulness meditation. Find a comfortable spot free from distractions, and set a five-minute timer.

1. Get Comfortable:
Sit in a comfortable position, keeping your back straight but relaxed. You can close or keep your eyes gently focused on a point before you.

2. Take a Few Deep Breaths:
Inhale deeply through your nose, allowing your abdomen to expand. Hold for a moment, then exhale slowly through your mouth. Repeat this a few times until you feel more relaxed.

3. Focus on Your Breath:
After a few deep breaths, allow your breathing to return to its natural rhythm. Focus on the sensation of your breath—the cool air entering your nostrils, the rise and fall of your chest or abdomen.

4. Notice Thoughts and Feelings:
As you settle into this space, thoughts and feelings may arise. Acknowledge them without judgment. You might think, "I'm feeling anxious," or "I'm a bit distracted." Instead of engaging with those thoughts, simply observe them. Imagine them as clouds passing in the sky, coming and going.

5. Gently Redirect Your Focus:

If you get caught up in thoughts, gently bring your focus back to
your breath. Inhale for a count of four, hold for a count of four and exhale for a count of four. Repeat this several times, allowing your mind to calm.

6. Gradual Return:

As your meditation ends, return your awareness to your surroundings. Notice the sounds, the feeling of the seat beneath you, and the space around you. When you feel ready, gently open your eyes and take a moment before moving back into your day.

Documenting the Experience:

After completing the meditation, take a moment to write about the experience in your journal. Here's a prompt to help guide your reflection:

- What did you notice about your thoughts and feelings during the meditation?
- Were there any moments of distraction or restlessness? How did you handle those?
- How did this short practice affect your mood or mindset moving forward?

Example Journal Entry:

Date: [Insert Date]

Experience:

Today's mindfulness practice helped me realize how quickly frustration can take hold of me. While waiting in line at the coffee shop, I felt impatience creeping in, but instead of letting it overwhelm me, I focused on my breath and observed my thoughts without judgment. Initially, I struggled with distracting thoughts about being late, but gently redirecting my focus to breathing brought a sense of calm.

After the meditation, I felt more centered. I was able to engage with the line more peacefully, reminding myself that everyone was in the same situation. I smiled at the barista even though she was slow, which felt like a huge shift from my earlier impatience.

I want to keep integrating this practice into my mornings. It feels empowering to experience my thoughts rather than react immediately.

Practicing this mindfulness meditation took Alex another step toward enhancing self-awareness and fostering resilience in facing life's challenges. The experience taught him that while he could not control external situations, he could control his reactions. The journey toward patience and perseverance was unfolding beautifully.

Embracing Control: Reactions Over Circumstances

AS ALEX continued his journey of self-discovery and personal growth, he grasped a pivotal truth: his life was often dictated not by external events but by his responses to those events. This realization marked a turning point in his approach to the challenges he faced, and it filled him with a sense of empowerment that had previously eluded him.

At the coffee shop, as Alex practiced mindfulness, he felt the familiar tides of impatience surge within him. The barista's slow pace and the long line seemed to conspire against his plans. Often, moments like these would spiral into frustration, and he would grumble internally or express annoyance outwardly. However, with his newfound mindfulness practice this time, he paused to reflect. He understood that the line was beyond his control—other people's pace, the limit of time, and even unforeseen circumstances like equipment malfunctions were all elements he had to accept.

The Power of Response

In realizing that he could not influence or speed up the flow of events around him, Alex felt a weight lift off his shoulders. This understanding allowed him to shift his focus inward. He could choose how to react, and therein lay his power. Instead of allowing the situation to define his mood and outlook, he concentrated on maintaining a calm demeanor.

This wasn't simply about forcing a positive attitude but about deeply engaging with the present moment. By practicing mindfulness, Alex learned to observe his thoughts and emotions without judgment. When frustration crept in, he acknowledged it as a natural response—a product of his human experience—but he didn't let it dictate his behavior. Instead, he embraced the practice of conscious breathing, letting the air fill his lungs and pushing out negativity with each exhale. He discovered that reacting patiently allowed him to preserve his energy and maintain a more balanced state of mind.

Building Emotional Resilience

The implications of this insight extended beyond the coffee shop. Alex also began to observe how this principle applied to his relationship with Mia. In moments of misunderstanding or disagreement, it was easy to fall into the trap of defensiveness. Miscommunication could easily lead to hurt feelings or escalating arguments, leaving both feeling drained and disconnected. However, Alex reminded himself that he couldn't control Mia's reactions or feelings—he could only control his responses.

When they faced conflicts, rather than doubling down on his perspective or getting upset when she seemed overwhelmed, Alex actively approached the situation patiently. He implemented the same mindfulness techniques he practiced that morning, focusing on listening to Mia without judgment. This helped him respond more thoughtfully, fostering open communication instead of defensiveness. He found that reacting with empathy and understanding reduced tension and created a safe space for them to express their feelings.

Transforming Challenges into Growth Opportunities

Through his daily situations, Alex shifted his perspective toward viewing challenges as opportunities for personal growth. Missing a train wasn't just an inconvenience but a moment to practice acceptance and adaptability. Instead of succumbing to frustration, Alex could reframe the experience as a chance to explore new paths—perhaps he could take a different route, discover a new café, or simply cherish a moment of unexpected downtime.

This newfound approach cultivated resilience. Alex learned that while he couldn't dictate the circumstances he faced, he could shape his journey through his chosen reactions. Assessing each situation patiently, he could cultivate an inner strength that made him more equipped to handle whatever life threw at him. Over time, this shift in mindset led to enhanced emotional intelligence, allowing him to navigate relationships and personal challenges with greater ease and grace.

The Ripple Effect of Mindful Reactions

As Alex embraced this transformative understanding, he noticed a ripple effect. His practice of mindful reactions not only improved his daily experiences but also inspired those around him. Friends and coworkers began to comment on his calm demeanor in stressful situations, and he found that modeling this behavior encouraged others to be more mindful of their responses. The sense of community that formed around this practice fostered deeper, more compassionate relationships, reinforcing the idea that personal growth is often intertwined with the evolution of our connections with others.

The journey through patience and perseverance became about personal achievement and contributing to a collective atmosphere of understanding and resilience. Alex's commitment to mastering his reactions transformed troubling situations into rich opportunities for growth for himself and those he cared about.

It was important to recognize that he could control his reactions. Alex now navigated life's complexities more easily and discovered a profound sense of agency and purpose. This realization was not the end of his journey but a powerful stepping stone toward becoming the resilient and mindful person he aspired to be.

Day 4: Embracing Discomfort

Story:

AS DAY 4 began, Alex felt a flutter of anxiety in his stomach. He had been putting off a difficult conversation with Mia for weeks, avoiding it like the plague. They had been experiencing some minor misunderstandings that, while seemingly small, had begun to create a rift in their communication. He knew that if they didn't address these issues, they could fester and lead to more significant problems.

With his new commitment to embracing discomfort and practicing patience, Alex decided it was time to tackle the conversation head-on. He reminded himself that the goal wasn't to win an argument but to understand Mia's perspective and communicate his feelings openly.

Preparing for the Conversation:

Before meeting Mia, Alex took some time to plan the conversation. He sat down in his favorite chair with a notebook and jotted down some key points for discussion. He also brainstormed ways to approach the topic sensitively.

Outline the Issues

Alex noted the specific instances that had caused misunderstandings. He wanted to express these clearly so Mia could understand his perspective.

Focus on Feelings

Instead of blaming or pointing fingers, Alex aimed to frame his feelings with "I" statements: "I feel concerned when…" or "I notice that I get anxious when…". This would help convey his feelings without making Mia feel attacked.

Set the Intention

Alex reminded himself of his intention: to listen actively and respond with patience. He practiced taking deep breaths and visualized a positive outcome, reassuring himself that open communication could strengthen their relationship.

The Conversation

Later that afternoon, as they sat down together in their cozy living room, Alex felt a mixture of nerves and determination. He initiated the conversation, expressing his desire to address some feelings. Mia listened attentively, and at first, the discussion flowed fairly well.

However, as the conversation progressed, it took an unexpected turn. Mia felt defensive about some of Alex's points, interpreting his concerns as criticism. He noticed her frustration rising despite Alex's commitment to constructive dialogue. Instead of the productive conversation he hoped for, it seemed to devolve into a heated exchange filled with misunderstandings.

Staying Composed

As tensions escalated, Alex felt the urge to react defensively. Memories of past arguments flashed in his mind, tempting him to fall into familiar patterns of frustration. But he remembered his intention to stay composed and patient.

Taking a deep breath, he paused and focused on listening. He consciously tried to hear what Mia was saying, seeking to understand her feelings rather than preparing his response. When Mia expressed her frustrations, Alex allowed her to talk without interruption, nodding and making eye contact to show that he was engaged.

At that moment of discomfort, Alex reminded himself that conversations don't always go as planned, but that didn't mean they lacked value. Even when challenges arise, it's essential to remain attentive and respectful. He continued to listen, offering verbal affirmations like "I understand" or "That makes sense" as she shared her feelings.

The Outcome

While the conversation didn't lead to an immediate resolution, Alex and Mia emerged with a clearer understanding of each other's perspectives. The discomfort of the moment transformed into an opportunity for growth. Alex felt pride for approaching the conversation with intent and patience, even when it was difficult.

After Mia shared her thoughts, Alex acknowledged her feelings and expressed his gratitude for her honesty. They agreed to continue the conversation at another time after both had a chance to reflect further.

Exercise: Planning Your Conversation

Now, it's your turn to embrace a conversation you've been avoiding. Here's how to approach it:

1. Identify the Conversation: Think about a conversation you've been putting off. Who is involved, and what topics do you need to address?
2. Prepare: Take a moment to write down your thoughts:
   - What specific issues do you want to discuss?
   - How can you frame your feelings using "I" statements?
   - What is your intention for the conversation? How do you want to feel at the end?
3. Practice Active Listening: During the conversation, focus on truly hearing what the other person is saying. Use non-verbal cues, maintain eye contact, and resist the urge to interrupt.
4. Reflect on the Outcome: After the conversation, take some time to journal about your feelings:
   - How did the conversation go? Did it unfold as you expected?
   - What emotions did you experience during and after the discussion?
   - What did you learn about yourself and the other person?
   - How can you apply these lessons in future conversations?

Example Journal Entry

Date: [Insert Date]
Conversation: [Brief description]
Outcome:
Today, I finally sat down with [Name] to discuss [topic]. I was nervous but prepared. I approached the conversation with intention and expressed my feelings through "I" statements.

Initially, things felt a bit tense, but I focused on listening to [Name] when they responded. I noticed myself getting defensive, but I took a deep breath and reminded myself to remain calm. We ended the conversation without a final resolution but understood each other better. I learned that it's okay for conversations not to go perfectly as long as there is an effort to communicate openly.

This experience taught me the importance of patience and active listening. I look forward to continuing this discussion and applying these lessons in future interactions.

Through this experience, Alex not only faced discomfort head-on but also learned that difficult conversations—while challenging—can lead to growth, understanding, and stronger relationships when approached with intention and care.

Day 5: Building Resilience Through Challenge

Story

ON DAY 5 of his journey, Alex felt excitement and a hint of trepidation. Inspired by his recent commitment to embrace discomfort, he set his sights on a physical challenge—a rigorous hike that wound through a nearby nature reserve. It was known for its scenic views, steep inclines, and demanding trails. Alex had always enjoyed hiking, but this particular trail pushed the boundaries of his endurance.

Waking up early, Alex packed his backpack with water, snacks, and a journal to capture his thoughts afterward. He reflected on how much he needed this challenge as he drove to the trailhead. He was eager to push his physical limits while also connecting with nature. More importantly, he recognized that this hike represented an opportunity to cultivate resilience.

The Hike: Confronting Limits

As he began the ascent, the initial excitement fueled his spirit. The crisp morning air invigorated him, and the beautiful scenery masked the physical strain. However, as the trail steepened, Alex quickly felt the burn in his legs and his heart pounding. Moments into the hike, doubt surfaced—what if he wasn't fit enough to finish? What if he had underestimated the challenge?

But instead of succumbing to the discomfort, Alex recalled his intention to embrace challenges as opportunities for growth. He concentrated on each step, reminding himself that pushing past his limits would lead to greater strength and resilience. He focused on breathing, deliberately inhaling and exhaling as he navigated the trail.

When fatigue set in, Alex took a moment to pause. He found a quiet spot near a towering rock and sat down to catch his breath. As he sat, he observed the beauty around him—the rustle of leaves, the distant sound of a waterfall, and the gentle chirping of birds. This moment of reflection reminded him that he was part of something more significant than his discomfort.

Pushing Through Fatigue

With renewed determination, Alex rose and continued the hike. Each step was challenging, but he found strength in perseverance. He set small milestones—taking a ten-step count before allowing himself to take a break or focusing on the next bend in the trail rather than the summit.

As he persisted, Alex began to feel a sense of accomplishment blossoming within him. It was exhilarating to realize that he could overcome the physical and mental hurdles before him. With every breath, he transformed fatigue into strength. The summit became less about the destination and more about the journey itself.

Finally reaching the top, Alex stood in awe of the breathtaking views. The landscape sprawled out before him—mountains, valleys, and the horizon stretching to infinity. He soaked at the moment, feeling a profound sense of achievement. Not only had he conquered the hike, but he had also confronted his self-doubt and pushed through discomfort. This experience reaffirmed a crucial lesson: growth happens outside the comfort zone.

Reflecting on the Experience

Sitting on the ledge overlooking the breathtaking panorama, Alex took a moment to reflect. He pulled out his journal and began to write about his experience:

Exercise: Embrace Your Challenge

Now it's your turn to build resilience through a physical challenge! Here's how to engage with this exercise:

1. Choose a New Physical Activity:
   - Think of an activity or hobby that you haven't tried before or that challenges you physically. This could be a hike, a new workout class, cycling, swimming, or even a dance session.
2. Set a Time Commitment:
   - Dedicate at least 30 minutes to this activity. Ensure you allow yourself to engage fully.
3. Focus on Perseverance:
   - Remember to focus on pushing through discomfort as you engage in this activity. Acknowledge the fatigue and any self-doubt that may arise, but allow yourself to push beyond those limits.
4. Reflect on Your Experience:
   - After your activity, take some time to process how you felt during and after:
     - What thoughts and feelings emerged as you confronted challenges?
     - Did you experience moments of doubt or fatigue? How did you handle those?

Liudmila Pirojenko

- What did you learn about your physical capabilities and mental resilience?
- How did this challenge shape your understanding of growth?

Example Journal Entry

Date: [Insert Date]
Activity: [Description of the activity you chose]
Reflection:
Today, I decided to challenge myself by [describe the activity, e.g., taking a yoga class, going for a long run, hiking a local trail]. As I started, I felt [describe initial feelings, e.g., excited, apprehensive, etc.].

During the activity, I struggled with [describe any physical discomfort or mental barriers faced]. However, I pushed through by focusing on [describe how you coped, such as breathing techniques, setting small milestones, or affirmations].

By the end, I felt [describe the outcome, e.g., exhausted, proud, invigorated, etc.]. This experience taught me how important it is to step outside my comfort zone. I realized that true growth happens when I challenge myself and confront my limits.

Alex built resilience and affirmed his ability to tackle difficulties head-on. This day served as a reminder that every step taken outside of comfort leads to self-discovery and personal growth. Embracing discomfort and pushing through limits is a cornerstone of building true resilience—something that will serve Alex in all areas of his life moving forward.

Day 6: The Power of Gratitude

Story

AS DAY 6 unfolded, Alex found himself in a reflective mood. After a week dedicated to embracing discomfort, confronting challenges, and developing resilience, he felt a newfound appreciation for his journey. He realized that patience was about waiting, recognizing, and being thankful for the lessons learned. Gratitude had become a vital part of his growth, illuminating the often-unnoticed moments that had helped him develop resilience.

Alex decided to sit down with his journal and list things he was grateful for. This exercise would ground his reflections, helping him see how each aspect of his life contributed to his ability to face challenges with patience and resolve.

Supportive Relationships

Alex thought about his friends and family who had been there for him during difficult times. Their encouragement and understanding gave him a solid foundation, reminding him that he didn't have to face challenges alone. This sense of community had strengthened his resilience.

Opportunities for Growth

He recalled the difficult conversations he had been avoiding and the courage it took to confront them. While initially daunting, those discussions led to deeper connections and better communication. Alex felt grateful for the lessons learned in vulnerability and honesty, which had expanded his emotional strength.

Personal Health and Well-being

Reflecting on his physical challenge from the previous day, Alex felt thankful for his body's ability to move and endure. The hike reminded him of the importance of physical health in building resilience. He recognized that taking care of himself physically allowed him to address emotional and mental challenges more effectively.

Mindfulness Practices

Alex thought about how he had started incorporating mindfulness and breathing exercises into his daily routine. These practices helped him navigate stressful situations with greater calmness and clarity. He was grateful for the mental tools that allowed him to respond with patience and intention rather than impulsively.

Nature's Beauty

Finally, Alex recalled the moments spent in nature during his hike and other outdoor activities. The beauty of the environment soothed his spirit, providing a comforting reminder of life's simple pleasures. He felt grateful that these experiences gave him peace and perspective amidst challenges.

After compiling his list, Alex felt lighter and more centered. Each item reminded him of how challenges often came hand in hand with growth and resilience. Gratitude, he realized, was a powerful tool in cultivating patience and transforming obstacles into opportunities for learning.

Exercise: Cultivating Gratitude

Now it's your turn to embrace the power of gratitude in your own life! Here's a simple exercise to help you focus on gratitude and reflect on your daily experiences:

- Write Down Five Things You're Grateful For:
- Reflect on your journey and consider five aspects of your life you appreciate. Think about how these relate to any challenges you've faced:
    - What are you grateful for?
    - How do these aspects contribute to your resilience or patience?
- Example List:
    - Supportive friends: Their encouragement has helped me stay motivated during challenging times.
    - New hobbies: Engaging in activities that push me out of my comfort zone has taught me valuable lessons about perseverance.
    - Access to nature: Being outdoors gives me peace and perspective when life feels overwhelming.
    - My health: I'm grateful for my body's ability to carry me through my daily challenges.
    - Mindfulness practices: They enable me to approach stressful situations with patience and greater clarity.

- Daily Reflection on Positivity: Each night, take a moment to list one positive experience from your day that required patience. This practice will help you recognize that patience often leads to rewarding experiences, allowing you to handle challenges gracefully.
- Example Reflection: Today's Positive Experience: I listened to a colleague's concerns about a project. Even though it was difficult to hear her frustrations, I practiced patience by allowing her to express herself fully. This deepened our relationship and resulted in a more productive collaboration afterward.

Alex strengthened his resolve and deepened his appreciation for the journey by acknowledging what he was grateful for and reflecting on moments requiring patience. This gratitude practice would become crucial to his ongoing development, reminding him that resilience is built on a foundation of patience, support, and reflection. Embracing gratitude would forever change how he viewed challenges, transforming them into opportunities for growth and deeper connections.

Day 7: Reflection and Moving Forward

Story

AS DAY 7 dawned, Alex woke up feeling a mix of accomplishment and anticipation. This week had been transformative—a journey through discomfort, resilience, gratitude, and self-discovery. He reflected on his challenges, the difficult conversations he had navigated, and the physical limits he had pushed. Each experience taught him important lessons about himself and reinforced his belief in the power of patience and perseverance.

Throughout the week, there were moments of doubt and exhaustion, but there were also moments of triumph that sparked joy and motivation. Alex felt renewed strength, recognizing that setbacks are often part of the journey. He took a moment to acknowledge his growth: he was no longer just going through the motions of his daily life; he was actively engaging in his development.

Committing to Continued Growth

Alex understood that this week was not just a one-time endeavor but the beginning of a lifelong commitment to personal growth. As he closed his eyes, he envisioned the practices he wanted to carry forward—embracing discomfort, practicing gratitude, and nurturing resilience. He decided it was essential to have a plan to keep building on these experiences.

Exercise: Letter to Yourself

Alex wrote a letter to himself to solidify his reflections and intentions moving forward. Here's what he penned:

Dear Alex,
As I reflect on this remarkable week, I want to take a moment to congratulate you on the commitment you've made to personal growth and resilience. You've faced challenges head-on, navigated difficult conversations, and embraced discomfort—each experience contributing to your strength and understanding of yourself.

Key Lessons Learned

1. Embracing Discomfort: You discovered that growth occurs outside your comfort zone. It's okay to feel uneasy when confronting challenges; those moments often lead to the most significant breakthroughs.
2. The Power of Patience: You learned that patience is not just about waiting—it's about understanding and appreciating the journey, even when things don't unfold as planned.
3. Gratitude as a Tool for Resilience: Recognizing what you are grateful for enhances your ability to persevere through tough times. Gratitude can shift your perspective and remind you of the supportive aspects of your life.

Steps to Continue Building Patience and Perseverance

1. Create a Daily Reflection Practice: Dedicate time each evening to write about one positive experience that required

patience. This will help you cultivate mindfulness and appreciate the small victories.

- Set Monthly Challenges: Continue pushing your limits by setting a new physical or personal challenge at the beginning of each month. This could be a new workout class, a personal development goal, or a creative project.
- Maintain Supportive Relationships: Regularly connect with friends and family who encourage and inspire you. Share your goals and challenges with them for accountability and support.
- Keep Practicing Mindfulness: Incorporate mindfulness techniques into your routine, such as meditation or breathing exercises, to stay grounded and better manage stress.

Journal Your Journey: Continue journaling your thoughts and reflections. This will help you process your experiences and provide insight into your growth.

Setting a New Challenge

For the coming month, I commit to participating in a community fitness class that pushes me physically and socially. This allows me to meet new people and immerse myself in a supportive environment that fosters resilience.

As this week concludes, remember that the journey of growth is ongoing. Each challenge faced, and lesson learned brings you closer to the person you aspire to be. Embrace every moment—both tough and joyful—and remind yourself that it's all part of the beautiful journey of life.

With gratitude and determination,

Alex

With the letter completed, Alex felt a weight lifted from his shoulders. It was a powerful affirmation of his growth and a roadmap for continued development. He understood that resilience is built over time, with each step taken leading to greater strength and readiness for whatever life might bring. By committing to these practices and embracing future challenges, Alex was excited to see where his journey would take him next.

Final Thoughts: The Journey Begins with Awareness

Alex felt a profound sense of clarity and empowerment as he stood after his transformative week. He understood that the journey of growth truly begins with the capacity to recognize the problems we face. In his case, the deep discomfort and emotional pain he experienced catalyzed change. This awareness sparked his journey—a signal that something was wrong and needed to be addressed.

Alex realized that acknowledging pain and discomfort is not a sign of weakness but the first courageous step toward transformation. Throughout the week, he learned to face his struggles head-on, using them as opportunities for reflection and growth. Each challenge he encountered, from difficult conversations to physical discomfort, taught him valuable lessons about resilience, patience, and gratitude.

He reflected that this journey is accessible to everyone but requires the willingness to recognize and confront our struggles. When we allow ourselves to feel the pain and discomfort, we open the door to profound personal growth. It's through this process of acknowledgment and confrontation that change becomes possible.

Encouragement for Others

With this insight, Alex felt compelled to encourage others to begin their awareness, healing, and transformation journeys. He recognized that everyone faces challenges in unique ways. Here are some thoughts for those who might be struggling:

1. Acknowledge Your Pain: Take a moment to reflect on what isn't working. What challenges and discomfort are you experiencing? Recognizing these feelings is the first step toward change.
2. Reflect on Your Experience: Write about your feelings and the situations that create discomfort. This can help clarify your thoughts and bring awareness to patterns that need addressing.
3. Seek Support: Don't hesitate to contact trusted friends, family, or professionals who can provide guidance and encouragement. Sharing your struggles can reduce their burden and foster connection.
4. Embrace the Discomfort: Understand that feeling discomfort is part of the process. It often signifies that you are on the brink of change and growth. Embrace it as a natural part of your journey.
5. Set Intentions for Change: Once you recognize the areas of discomfort, outline specific steps you can take to address them. Commit to creating a plan that includes challenges that allow for personal development.

Alex's journey demonstrated that recognizing pain and discomfort is not the end but the beginning of a powerful transformation. These very moments can lead us to deeper understanding and self-discovery. As Alex moves forward, he remains committed to his practices, ready to face new challenges with an empowered spirit and a heart of gratitude.

To anyone reading this, your journey also begins with awareness. Embrace the pain, acknowledge what isn't right, and let it guide you toward positive change. You have the strength within you to transform your struggles into stepping stones, paving the way for a resilient and fulfilling life.

Your journey awaits—start today!

Disclaimer Notice

The information in this document is for educational and entertainment purposes only.

All efforts have been made to show accurate, up-to-date, reliable, and complete information. No warranties of any kind are declared or implied. I just wanted to let you know that the author is not engaged in rendering legal, financial, medical, or professional advice. The content within this book has been derived from various sources. Please look at a licensed professional before you try any techniques outlined in this book. This book was crafted using AI technology to enhance clarity, research, and content organization.

Liudmila Pirojenko

COULD YOU TAKE A MOMENT TO SHARE YOUR THOUGHTS IN A REVIEW?

I would be incredibly grateful
It truly helps

Author Bio

LIUDMILA PIROJENKO, LIUDMILA PIROJENKO, MA in Languages, is a Teacher and Translator. Due to the specifics of her profession, she often has to deal with the problems presented in this book Contact: LinkedIn account https://www.linkedin.com/in/liud mila-pir/

Travel Italy Newsletter: https://exegi.substack.com/
Mystery in Life Newsletter https://mystery-life.beehiiv.com

For Reviews, please visit
Amazon Author's Page
https://www.amazon.com/stores/Liudmila-
Pirojenko/author/B0DK91G1JW

9 7 9 8 3 0 3 7 4 2 0 8 6